II 12 13 14 15 16 17 18 1920

For Gabriel Claudio Marzollo.
Here's to love, laughter, and learning.
—J. M.

For Macie Lynn Phillips.
May education be your strongest weapon.
—C. P.

Text copyright © 2011 by Jean Marzollo
Photographs copyright © 2011 by Chad Phillips
All Rights Reserved
HOLIDAY HOUSE is registered in the U.S. Patent and Trademark Office.
Printed and Bound in April 2011 at Tien Wah Press, Johor Bahru, Johor, Malaysia.
www.holidayhouse.com
First Edition
1 3 5 7 9 10 8 6 4 2

Library of Congress Cataloging-in-Publication Data
Marzollo, Jean.
Help me learn numbers 0-20 // by Jean Marzollo; photographs by Chad Phillips. — 1st American ed.
p. cm.
ISBN 978-0-8234-2334-7 (hardcover)
1. Numbers, Natural—Juvenile literature. 2. Numeration—Juvenile literature.
3. Counting—Juvenile literature. I. Phillips, Chad, ill. II. Title.
QA141.M34 2011
513.2'11—dc22
2010029892

Help Me Learn Numbers 0–20

by Jean Marzollo

photographs by Chad Phillips

Holiday House / New York

O

Not one thing.
This box is clear-o.
How many inside?
I count _____ (zero).

Walking, walking,
just for fun.
How many rabbits?
I count _____ (one).

2

Oink! Oink!
Who are you?
How many piggies?
I count _____ (two).

3

How many fish
do I see?
I see one,
two, _____ (three).

4

Take one truck.
Add three more.
How many are there?
I count _____ (four).

5

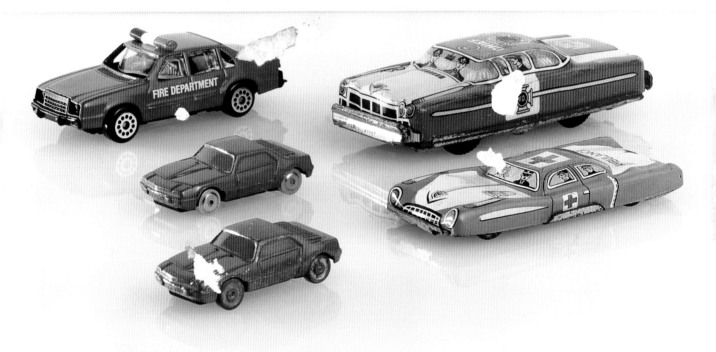

Count the cars
you'll take for a drive.
I'll take
1, 2, 3, 4, _____ (five).

6

Little, busy
duck and chicks.
How many are you?
We are _____ (six).

7

This number loves
to rhyme with eleven.
How many are you?
We are _____ (seven).

8

Count the deer.
(Aren't they great?)
1, 2, 3, 4,
5, 6, 7, _____ (eight).

9

Gingerbread faces
all in a line.
How many are there?
I count _____ (nine).

10

One poodle, four swans,
five mice, and when . . .
you count all the animals,
you'll get to _____ (ten).

This number loves
to rhyme with seven.
When you count all the ducklings,
you'll get to _____ (eleven).

12

Can you tell me
where to shelve
Mr. Rooster?
Box _____ (twelve).

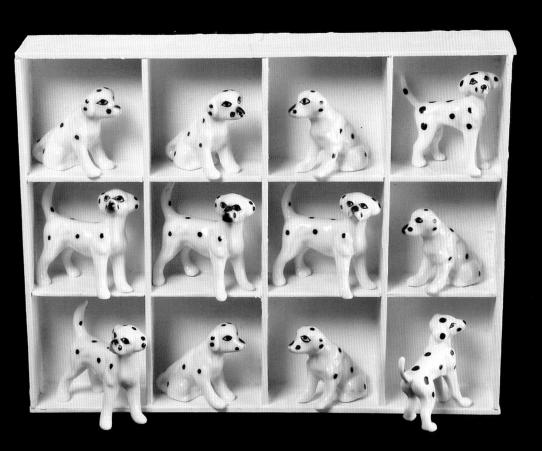

Arf! We're cute.
Arf! We're clean.
We're Dalmatians!
We're _____ (thirteen).

14

Please don't count
the tangerine.
How many apples
in all? _____ (fourteen).

Ducks afloat
on a tambourine.
How many
can you count? _____ (fifteen).

16

We are monsters!
We are mean!
How many are we?
We're _____ (sixteen).

Our scary faces
can't be seen.
How many are
we now? _____ (seventeen).

18

Yellow, red, blue, and green. How many people in boats? _____ (eighteen).

19

How many people
are in this scene?
Can you count
up to _____ (nineteen)?

20

Ten pairs of earrings.
That is plenty.
When you count ALL the earrings,
you'll get to _____ (twenty).

0

1 2

3 4 5

6 7 8 9

10 11 12 13 14

15 16 17 18 19 20

What's your favorite
number today?
Name it. Touch it.
Say *Hooray*!

Dear Parents and Teachers,

The purpose of this book is to help young children enjoy learning numbers and number value so that they will be ready to succeed in kindergarten today.

Based on the Common Core State Standards, kindergarten children, by the end of the school year, are expected to count as high as 20 and to answer questions that ask "How many?" As the children count, they are expected to mentally connect each number with one and only one object. They are also expected to understand that the last number said is the answer to the question "How many?"

Start your child on the path to math at an early age. One- and two-year-olds will enjoy the pictures and rhymes in this book. As your child grows, hold your child's finger lightly and touch the objects as you count them. (This helps children make the one-to-one connection.) At some point, if you pause at the end of each verse, your child will finish it with the number answer. The rhyme is a clue.

Older children may memorize the rhymes and like to read or pretend to read them to you.

Help your child count playthings and other familiar objects. Don't overdo it. Make it fun.

Feel proud that you are starting your child down the path to math!

Happy counting,
Jean Marzollo

Grateful Thanks

We would like to thank Grace Wilkie, Tandy Scholar and past president, Association of Mathematics Teachers of New York State. Grace helped us understand the Common Core Standards. As Grace explained to us, "It's important today to assist our pre-kindergarten and kindergarten parents and teachers with fun and interesting books that relate to the Mathematics Standards. Having the opportunity to learn and appreciate mathematics at a young age sets a child's foundation for years."

To learn more about these standards, please go to: www.corestandards.org.

We would also like to thank Grace Maccarone, our editor, and Claire Counihan, our art director, at Holiday House for being so enthusiastic about this book right from the start.

We'd like to thank Mimi Whitson, Cassie Traina, and Ali Phillips for painting the little wooden peg people. We'd like to thank Claudio Marzollo for building the shelves for the Dalmatians and Susan Jeffers for her ongoing support.

We would like to thank Bob and Barbara Wade of Once Upon A Time Antiques in Cold Spring, New York. Their wonderful toy store is where we found the dogs, pigs, fish, deer, swans, and other animals for the book. We thank Archie McPhee & Co. for giving us permission to put the Finger Monsters (we think you can figure out which ones they are) in the book, and we thank Virginia Bjorgum of Nature's Accents for giving permission to put the Brushkins (posing for #7) in the book. Have we missed anyone? If so, let us know, and please forgive us.

Jean Marzollo and Chad Phillips

Numbers, numbers.
Here they are.
Each one you count
makes you a star!

Numbers, numbers,
look alive!
Can you count
the stars by five?

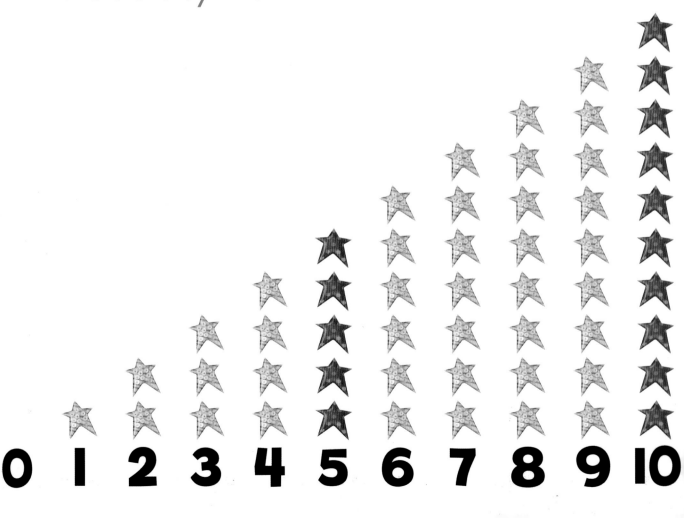

0 1 2 3 4 5 6 7 8 9 10